Dear Family and Friends of Young Readers,

Learning to read is one of the most important milestones your child will ever attain. Early reading is hard work, but you can make it easier with Hello Readers.

Just like learning to play a sport or an instrument, learning to read requires many opportunities to work on skills. However, you have to get in the game or experience real music to keep interested and motivated. Hello Readers are carefully structured to provide the right level of text for practice and great stories for experiencing the fun of reading.

Try these activities:

• Reading starts with the alphabet and at the earliest level, you may encourage your child to focus on the sounds of letters in words and sounding out words. With more experienced readers, focus on how words are spelled. Be word watchers!

• Go beyond the book — talk about the story, how it compares with other stories, and what your child likes about it.

• Comprehension — did your child get it? Have your child retell the story or answer questions you may ask about it.

Another thing children learn to do at this age is learn to ride a bike. You put training wheels on to help them in the beginning and guide the bike from behind. Hello Readers help you support your child and then you get to watch them take off as skilled readers.

— Francie Alexander
  Chief Academic Officer,
  Scholastic Education

D1511954

For Aaron
— E.D.

Best wishes and regards to
Vincent and Raymond
— M.S.

ISBN 0-439-43964-7

12 11 10 9 8 7 6 5 4 3 2   4 5 6 7 8/0

Printed in the U.S.A.
First printing, March 2003

Grow Tree, Grow!

by Ellen Dreyer
Illustrated by Maggie Swanson

Hello Reader! Science — Level 1

SCHOLASTIC INC.

New York   Toronto   London   Auckland   Sydney
Mexico City   New Delhi   Hong Kong   Buenos Aires

Once I was an acorn.

I sent my roots into the ground.

Soon I was a tiny seedling.
The sun gave my green leaves energy
to grow.

My little roots drank the rain.

I became a sapling.

Now I am a tree.

In spring, I grow leaves
and acorns.
Squirrels nibble on my acorns.

Birds lay eggs in nests that I hold up high.

In the hot summer, my big branches give cool shade.

My leaves change color
when autumn comes.

Now my leaves are as dry as paper
and begin to fall.
My acorns drop, too.

Will they become trees someday?

Winter comes.
Snow and ice cover
my branches.
I rest.

The whole forest sleeps.

Then one day, the snow and ice melt.
My tiny buds turn into leaves.

Down below on the ground
are tiny seedlings.
Together we all make a forest.

In a few months, there will be
fall leaves again.